The Best You

Calm Down

Dona Herweck Rice

Consultants

Diana Herweck, Psy.D.

Publishing Credits

Rachelle Cracchiolo, M.S.Ed., *Publisher*
Conni Medina, M.A.Ed., *Managing Editor*
Nika Fabienke, Ed.D., *Series Developer*
June Kikuchi, *Content Director*
John Leach, *Assistant Editor*
Kevin Pham, *Graphic Designer*

Image Credits: All images from iStock and/or Shutterstock.

Library of Congress Cataloging-in-Publication Data

Names: Rice, Dona, author.
Title: The best you : calm down / Dona Herweck Rice.
Description: Huntington Beach, CA : Teacher Created Materials, [2018] | Audience: K to Grade 3.
Identifiers: LCCN 2017026885 (print) | LCCN 2017055056 (ebook) | ISBN 9781425853334 (eBook) | ISBN 9781425849597 (pbk.)
Subjects: LCSH: Calmness--Juvenile literature. | Emotions--Juvenile literature.
Classification: LCC BF575.C35 (ebook) | LCC BF575.C35 R53 2018 (print) | DDC 155.42/4247--dc23

Teacher Created Materials
5301 Oceanus Drive
Huntington Beach, CA 92649-1030
http://www.tcmpub.com

ISBN 978-1-4258-4959-7

Printed by: 51497
Printed in: China

Table of Contents

Angry!

Your breathing speeds up and you feel **flushed** and warm.
Your hands close into fists.

You want to yell.
What is happening to you?
You feel angry!

In Charge

Everyone feels angry at times.
Anger is a normal feeling.
You can choose what to do about it.

You are in charge of your feelings.
Your feelings are not in charge of you.

When you are angry, some choices make you feel better.
Some choices make you feel worse.

Having a **tantrum** is not okay. You might hurt others. What can you do to feel better?

Make Good Choices

There are many good choices you can make when you feel angry.

The next pages are filled with ideas for you to try. Try them, and see what works best for you!

Breathing

One easy way to calm down is to take deep breaths.
You can do this anywhere.

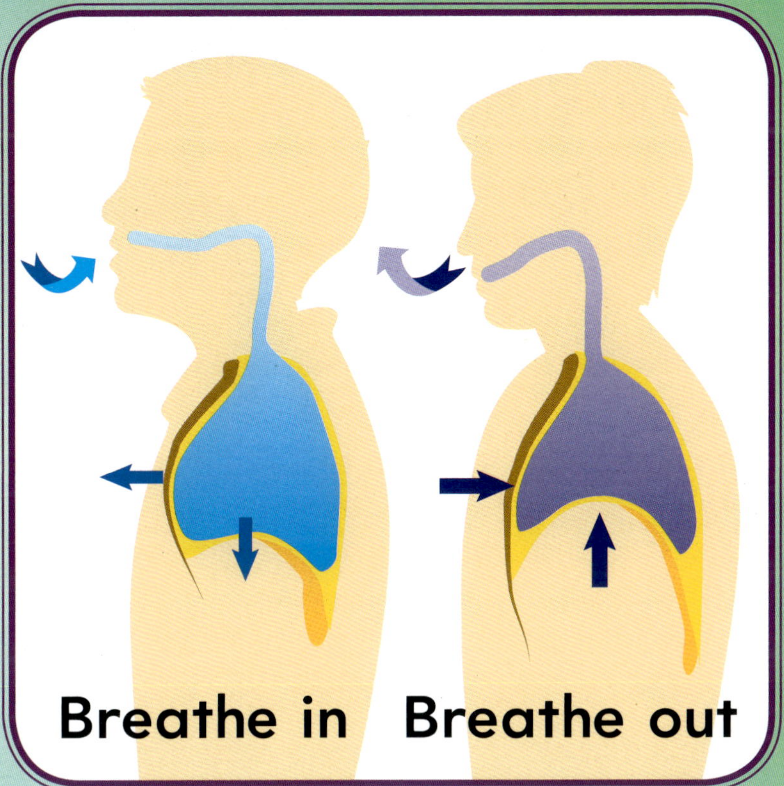

Breathe in slowly through your nose and out through your mouth.
Do this a few times until you start to calm down.

Self-Talk

Self-talk is also easy to do.
Talk to yourself about being calm.
Use a **gentle** tone.

Say to yourself, "Calm down." Say, "Everything will be okay." You do not need to say these things out loud.

Counting

Counting from 1 to 10 works for many people. That is all it takes.

Count slowly.
This may help you calm down.
If you need to, count to 10 again.

Running

Do you like to run? Running is a great thing to do when you feel angry.

Running can help you calm down. Running is also good for you!

Yoga

Many types of exercise help you calm down. Yoga is a good choice.

In yoga, you form your body into shapes. You hold each shape for a while. You breathe calmly.

You Can Do It!

It is not wrong to feel angry. Calming down is the best choice for you and everyone around you.

You can do it.
Remember that you are
in charge of you!

Glossary

flushed

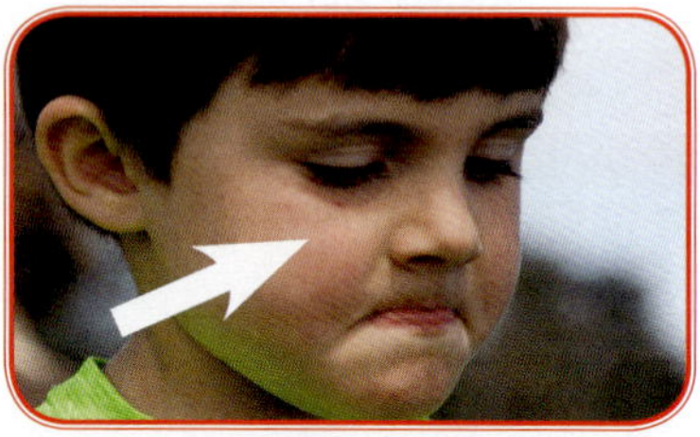

gentle

self-talk

tantrum

yoga